Unlacing

Ten Irish-American Women Poets

Unlacing

Ten Irish-American
Women Poets

Edited by
Patricia Monaghan

Fireweed Press
Fairbanks, Alaska

Unlacings: Ten Irish-American Women Poets

Thanks to the following people for assistance in the production of this book: Roland Wulbert, Jane Hixon, Bill Connor, Kathy Marchlinski, Knute Skinner, Jerah Chadwick and the Feminist Wrters Guild.

Table of Contents

Introduction
Patricia Monaghan

When the Irish-American literary tradition is charted, it looks rather like a pub in the old country. Finley Peter Dunne is there, and James Farrell with him. Eugene O'Neill drops in, as does F. Scott Fitzgerald and John O'Hara. A couple of the new lads--William Kennedy, John Gregory Dunne--make a showing. It's a place for the boys to get away from the world of women, and where the woman who shows her head outside a "snug" is no lady.

On special occasions Mary McCarthy is let in for a round, or Kay Boyle, or Mary Gordon. But the image of the Irish-American writer as a hard-drinking, priest- and mother-ridden *puer aeterna* doesn't leave much room for them or others of our sex. Irish-American women poets, searching for literary roots, find no acknowledged tradition here from which to draw.

The ten women poets in this volume have dealt with this lack by returning to Ireland--literally, spiritually, or both. Failing to find a tradition in our real homeland, we look across the water to the land of our grandmothers. Grandmothers abound in the work of Irish-American women--McKiernan, Callaway, Blanchard, Swander. The last family member to have been rooted in the old world, she is also the one who cut ties to home and family to explore a new one. The Irish-American poet gazing from this side of the ocean at Ireland meets the memory of her grandmother's gaze, yearing and fearing towards America. In the grandmother, the Irish-American poet sees something of herself, tied to home and kin yet compelled to wander in search of freedom and fullness.

Fullness, and its opposite, also haunts these poets. Famine--the Famine--hangs in the past of the Irish-American woman poet more powerfully than in that of her brothers, for starvation is, to women of this century, a powerful metaphor for the female spirit's yearning and hunger for a freedom society denies. Like Eavon Boland in Ireland, Margaret Blanchard in America finds in tales of the Great Hunger a compelling question about spiritual need. Nancy

1

Sarah Schoellkopf describes a passion for art in terms of food and lust; Katherine McNamara charts sexual obsession in terms of carnivores hunting.

Just as The Hunger of Ireland's past presents a vivid image for the hungers of today's woman, so the conflict that continues in Ireland today provides a rich and complex image. The poet finds, through this heritage, a common ground with revolutionaries of other lands, as does Renny Golden in her poems to rebels in Central and South America. Or she discovers the rebel in herself, in her dreams, in her actions. Or she makes common cause with the victims in ravaged countries, as Eithna McKiernan does in recalling the experiences of the bereaved of My Lai and Chernobyl.

Historical Ireland provides three great images to the Irish American: grand-mother, hunger, war. But there is something else in these poems, something prehistoric, something from that Ireland Edna O'Brien calls "A Pagan Place." From this land of myth and magic and sensuality, the Irish-American poet draws the greatest richnesses. Nuala Archer chants like an *ollav* of the ancient Hag of Beare come to America to reappear as the Coyote of the indigenous people; she sings of the marvels of technology with a vision of true magic behind them. Nancy Schoellkopf, too, finds connections between the spirituality of ancient Celts and that of indigenous Americans, connecting through the California Indians with the spiritual perceptions of her forebears across the waters.

These women poets share a deep, a pagan, sensuousness towards land, to-wards children, towards lovers, towards language. Sometimes this sensuous-ness is confined in the family, tied to kin and home, as in Tess Gallagher's des-cription of a man washing his dying mother. Sometimes it is lawless, rebellious, outside society, as it is to McKiernan's "other woman." In this poetry, holiness breaks through the senses and unties us from a stony lovelessness. Over and over, each by herself, we find the same images for this encounter. We repeat the magic words, the primal sounds: *stone, sea, flesh, green, horses, boat, birds.* In the poetry of this encounter with the force of life through--not beyond--the body, is the essence of Irish-American women's poetry.

2

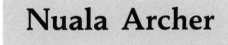

Nuala Archer

The Lost Glove Is Happy

Is it in the terminal I left
the brown, rabbit-fur-lined gloves
made in Taiwan? Gloves
I've worn in Ireland.
Gloves that kept my fingers
warm walking the bitter cold
coastline of Bull Island
with Howth and her necklace
of lights in the background.
Gloves lost now between Stillwater,
Oklahoma and Lubbock, Texas
on the way to see my mother.

"Come," she said. "I'm in
the midst of desolation. Come.
Take Southwest Airlines, past
Love Field. I'll be waiting
for you. I'll be waiting."

And in the mall, when I got
to Lubbock, arrived to embrace
my mother in desolation, she had
me strip, try on outfit
after outfit -- sweaters, trousers,
skirts, shirts, shorts, slips
and blouses -- to see like
Mary, Mary, quite contrary,
how does your garden, my garden,

grow? She in her mid-fifties
and me at the cliff-edge of
twenty-nine. My mother had me
fly to Lubbock and on the way
I lost my rabbit-
fur-lined gloves. When I got

there, when I arrived, when
I reached desolation, my mother
alone, in the middle of crazy
cottonfields, my mother in
desolation, I reached her,
I travelled to her,
to desolation, and in desolation
we were as lost as any
two mismatched gloves and
for a few moments we relaxed, lost
and strangely happy,
in the Lubbock Mall, without
labels, stripped to our bones.

A Breaking, A Bread-Colored Light

Then Anne who is also
Ruth, and Nuala who
is also Miriam, came to me
as I lay curled in the ear
of a seashell. And Anne,
also Ruth, unlaced
my shoes and let them slip
to the sand of the black sea-
bed. She cradled and
kissed each step of my tired
feet while Nuala,
also Miriam, tenderly ran
her fingers through my hair
like a lover
calming my roots, combing
my broken ends.

          And to their
coming I called back: "You
are my two girls. My always-
and-for-never two girls. Ruth,
also Miriam. And Nuala, also
Anne." And they lifted me up
then to the high boats
of their silence, their
beautiful bodies, and in

the boats of their bones, into
the breaking bread-colored
light, we set sail, we broke
free, we gave thanks.

Between Swilly And Sewanee

--for Naomi

Who is the mother of these words? Nonsense syllables
leaping up between Swilly and Sewanee. Three-
thousand miles of ocean: "O, bring back, bring

back:" Lovers crossing-over: winging the never-
forever gap, the Atlantic assemblage: her mother
and my mother and myself: "Make me as I am --

make me beautiful." Each with the wind of watery
trees in our faces and faith in the following dolphins --
bowing and breathing-in dawn's opal brilliance,

the colostrum of our comings. Barking like Blueticks
for the sun, curling into the Q.E. II, the dolphins are
the clouds at my window, nuzzling the green stillness

of flight -- as if the third leavetaking were a coda,
another Rosetta story -- finally cracked. In the wavering
hyphens-- a home between homes-- a liquid blossoming of

bones -- a zany confluence: the Darien pivoting in Dublin --
to a fleche, a matinee of sheer quiet. Pine and palm tracks
merging. A life glowing in a mot of otherly swayings.

Train Trance: Paper City

That they blow down our streets,
can be found in all rivers,

and like kites, re-leaf the winter
trees, is by now a cliche.

Wind from the sea turns a page.
Print, like butterfly dust, powders

the fingers. But there is more
than meets the headlines.

The tangerine tree beginning to
fruit (6th edition) is a gracious

corollary to the moment just
after this photograph: the girl,

dot-to-dot, imaged here, in the rub-
ble of Summerhill, is caught on

film. Click. Click. I descend
from the commuter's track. Black

my whorls and mazes with the rub-
off inky alphabet, the scarecrow bits

of news, the transfer of her name.
I hear the glass the girl lets fly.

The splinter in my eye. Rubbish!
The vandalism of breaking light.

Brown Electric Blanket

The coyote is singing, Do you
    know there is an open door
    what are you hoping for
  an open door, an open door
    what are you
    what are you
  an open door hoping for?
The coyote just out of the bathtub
    is singing.   She is wet and singing and
    splashing herself dry with a pink towel.
  The coffee in the voluptuous two-tiered
    Pamela pot is bubbling
    like a brown mud geyser, flowering
brown and out-of-focus, a flowering
    of farts, syncopating, like brown
    Backgammon stones gone bonkers.
  Outside the Black-capped Chickadee
    is throwing up her eyes into air,
    throwing up her eyes
high into trees, the Chickadee is
    throwing up her eyes
    and catching them again. Again and
  again her rocketing eyes fall into
    the black rose-hole of her
    empty sockets. Do you know?
Do you know? You do? You too?
    Some days it is almost impossible
    to un-nest the brown clicking

blanket from around this body
　　broken beautifully with bones,
　　to un-nest the blanket and
to rest easy, knowing that the worries
　　of the day, day in Oklahoma,
　　homa, are still waiting,
　restless as rattlers.

　　The Hag of Beare is a bear
　　or a blink or a birthplace.
A pronoun or a potato.
　　The Hag of Beare is a relative speed,
　　a verbal rhythm sketching
　lightly her lacy vegetables and
　　embroideries, in indefinite quantities,
　　into the river-mouth of my dreams
and some days it is almost
　　impossible to un-nest
　　from the brown, clicking, electric blanket
　clicking lightly and luring me,
　　luring me to the reverse
　　rioting light of her knocking. The Hag
of Beare is knocking. Do you hear
　　her knocking?
　　And the Canadian geese?
　And the monarchs fluttering
　　through Elk City, through the tennis
　　courts bubbling with green balls
and bronzed bodies? The butterflies,
　　buddhas of cinnamon with batteries

13

enough to send Brazil reeling.
The Hag of Beare sleeps through my catastrophes
and is knocking me into a sea,
a cornucopia of cinnamon,
a contradiction in green.
The Hag of Beare is from the Purple Bogs
of Ireland and she has lost
her deep fear of losing
boundaries, even the bog. She is
from the bog, that plenitude, boundless as

the coyote, bare-bottomed, just out of the bath.
How was I to know she was
a woman and singing? That Hag, do you
know my Chickadees, and can I tell you?
Can I? Can I tell you?
Can I tell you? I tell you, my
Chickadees, that some days it is almost impossible:
The clicking electric blanket lures talk
of trees, talk of that knocking,
talk of that tender sketching,
that tension of bedside reading,
that rioting light un-nesting me?

Margaret
Blanchard

Before the Hunger: Megan's Blessing

as she prepares a meal for the other nuns

What an awful dream,
potatoes becoming stones
as we pulled them out of the earth,
hardening in our hands like mud,
turning white,
round, smooth like bones.
And when we put them in the fire
to cook, they cracked.

Thank God the potatoes
in this sack are still alive.
Aren't you a beauty?
Earth still clings to you,
precious root,
who grew inside her womb.
After you were pulled from her,
she let you go reluctantly.

Let me hold you up for blessing
as the priest does the sacred bread.
Please don't turn to stone,
faithful old soul,
our staff, our life, God's special
gift to us, brown
and simple as we've become
since they stripped us of our trees,
hidden underground as we've been

since they stole the surface from us
and taxed us for standing on it.
Like our heart which beats on unseen
you nourish us, feeding all.
Your blind eyes have seen
greener days and richer soil
like ours which now see more
than they dare tell.

They call you plain, even
ugly, but we know the grace
which comes through you,
as fully as in their fancy
foods, as cleanly as though
our own sweat, not someone
else's blood.

God's spirit unites you
even as I chop you apart,
so after we plant your pieces
you can become whole again--
not once or twice but many times,
loaves and fishes multiplied.
Into the pot now go
to mingle with the other
wonders of creation,
carrot, onion, cabbage.
Oh Lord, we need look no further
than a stew to witness
your glory.

One Who Knew, 1839: Kathleen's Vision
which causes her, at the age of 70, to stop eating

How to tell of my refusal?
How I rue the day I was born with this gift
which seems more a curse, to see a future
I'll be no part of, but even worse,
one where there will be
living corpses in the roads
with hollow, haunted faces
and we'll have no food to give them.

God's ways are strange.
Fat times we never question,
but come the lean, and we must
complain: why should He test
our country so?
We're in the holiest of company;
His own son died at the hands of
Roman thieves away from their own
homes, bleeding his country dry
to feed their baser needs.

Get too far from home, I say,
you become a stranger to yourself.
Extend the roots too far
and they get stringy,
strangling your best growth,
leaving you tight-fisted.
Such human meanness isn't

God's fault.
He gave us this natural rhythm
of give and get, have
and have not, empty and full,
that we see in the seasons
of the year, in the earth's
generosity in summer, her need
to rest in winter. We see this in our
own breathing, as we take in
and let out.

If we hold on too long,
like the rich with money,
or can't get enough, like the poor,
we all won't survive.
 If we hold onto
food, it rots;
if we stuff ourselves,
we grow ill. A body must let go
the air it breathes and the food
it eats, just as the earth must
let go her fruits and flowers
each fall so more can grow
next spring.

Now's my time for letting go.
We come into life with clenched fists
and grow by holding on,
but we leave it with open,
empty hands.

I cannot bear
to look ahead and see
children clutching dead mothers,
crying for food,
mothers holding bodies
of children who grew
too weak to eat.
I cannot see all this without
choking. How can I, who've
lived my life to the full,
eat up the extra?

Let me be one less
mouth to feed.
Let the young eat and grow strong
enough to face the bad times
with all the courage they
can raise.
I won't be here to bear it
then, so I suffer it now.

God's mercy in this:
appetite is gone;
lightness is all
that's left to feel.

The Way Over, 1840: Rose's Lament
on the deck, out of steerage

At last I can breathe
without taking in the stench as well.
Dead Lord, why couldn't I guess
with a name like mine
I wasn't meant to travel?
Oh why didn't I
leave my roots
in the old sod--
let myself spin out
the rest of my days
blooming and fading?
Here I am,
a withered bush
baked hard and dry
by fever's searing grasp.
Now an empty bowl,
I 'm a burden
rather than a blessing.

Before me stretches the eternal blue
of sea meeting sky
where I once so longed to sail.
Behind me the green rolling hills,
the wandering walls,
mist in the morning,
goat in the meadow,
the meandering stream,

the gypsy wagon,
the companionable loom,
the heart's fire,
my feet on the rough floor.

What's wrong with me?
I can see my head's
on backwards,
but better a glimpse
of the new world
than that dull knowing
all-there-is-to-see.
   How dizzy I'm getting with this fresh air.
   Let me sit on that circle of rope
   and wait till I clear.

Please don't let me die yet.
   Mama, are you listening?
   Come put your soft cheek next to mine
   and let me feel you smile.
And Molly, sister, let us hug--
our admiration no longer envy
we have to hide--
   no more holding back,
   as in the fearful rush
   with which we parted.

Ah, hear that sweet music, as if Sean
himself were on the deck,
playing his melancholy ditty

as only a young man dare,
   nostalgia and desire balanced,
   memory and longing poised,
while I, consumed by homesickness, wait
to curl up like an old shell
on the new shore,
indifferent to its fate,
whether empty or full,
tumbling back into the waves
to be sucked back
into the terrible ocean...
oh, too late,
too late.

Out there on the sea an old woman beckons,
points towards a light on the horizon.
A cloud gathering?
The moon rising?
Dawn?
The new world?

I curl into this round nest
of rope
to rest
and sail
out to meet the moon.

        (Born 1788, Ireland; died 1840, at sea.)

The Convent, 1900: Eileen's Choice

I'm sorry, so sorry, dear
lord, I cannot follow
your call, as the sheep
the shepherd. More like the fox
we tried once to tame,
I long to rush into the woods
without even a glance
back at the rigid
bars, pin-hole
vistas, constraining
rules which trap me here.
Fled is the simple
faith which led
along this narrow way,
much like the trail
west across the plains,
where one got lost forever
if she strayed.

Please don't abandon
me now as I forsake
your holiest path. The woods
are full of threats:
excommunication if they
forbid me to leave; the shame of
my family; the cage of
spinsterhood or the restraints
of marriage, the pit

of heathenism.
Like an unblazed trail, the path out
is crooked, steep. One slip,
far from this comfortable
prison, and I could fall
to even worse: the mire
of lost souls.
       Holy Mary, don't
let them cast me out
of our mother the Church.
Please don't let
this be a mistake
I'll live the rest
of my days regretting.

Soon I must chose.
I don't care it's never
been done before; it's the first
and only time for me too.
Once we've embraced the future
as she leaves her touch on us.
As the century
turns, for better or
worse, I begin to move.

Kathy Callaway

Carrie Usher's Journal

Her rush to finish it,
twenty scrawled pages in pencil.
You were seven, mother,
watched the uneven loops unfold
on the paper tablet. She wrote with her left hand,
right arm blackening to the shoulder.
In the end she took your name away: *Omah*
she'd called you, from the Sioux
those who go upstream or against the wind.
She was afraid for you. The bare house leaned
into the tamaracks. Wild rice on the lake
bowed down in waves.

To make room for you, her sister
gave away a daughter. You paid for it,
scrubbed everything and tried to be small,
thought about your dead parents, missing pages,
my name is, my name is--
history blowing away like chaff.
You ran to the next house
but there were children in chains there.

For many years you checked and checked
stone markers. I'm writing to tell you
I have found the journal,
it's stained like an old map, and over the landmass
your mother's writing leans like Conestogas--
clear, windblown, so hopeful--there are cattle

belly-deep in prairie grass,
a Cedar River settlement, Misquakee playmates.
Long wagons north when she was ten, her father
singing, hiding whiskey from his brother.
Their open laughter--

She ran whole summers behind him,
wore the same print dress, hair cropped
to save combing. He called her *Dutchy,* they fished
like the Crow. In winter she walked miles,
feet bound in burlap, taught the blacksmith
to write "horseshoe" and "sled-runner"
under the simple drawings in his tally book.
At sixteen a certified teacher.
She had a vision in a yellow clearing--
kneeling down, she writes, *I thanked God for so
rewarding me.* Her mother waiting for her,
hands wrapped in a fading apron.

It ends with her father's wagon mired
on a corduroy road. You call me
by my own name now, it's *daughter,* the word
falling through these pages like tracks
on a pine-forest floor,
prints disappearing behind the walker.

Three-Day New Year, Soldotna, Alaska

Daughter of the last chief
of the Kenai Athabascans,
she's here with her Irish husband,
two grown girls, a son.
My relatives press around them.
Smaller children steal mukluks,
mittens, scarves. Her daughters are tall,
wear black silk over their collarbones.
One is engaged, and has a choker that says "Equal."
The other is handsome as a mare,
leans wholly against the side of my
brother-in-law-by-marriage. A Polaroid whirs.
Her girls are loosely posing in their bodies.
Not one son in either family can read--
dream-faced, lucid hunters,
they will tangle and struggle for hours
in front of the television.

Her tribe is rich, incorporated,
negotiates as a separate nation.
She hands out gifts like a diplomat,
black hair steel-blue under the kitchen light.
As we pull around the table someone tells me:
Don't ask about native land-claims.
We drink Prinz Brau, Schnapps, Tia Maria,
laugh at old jokes and at her husband who plays
Mad Pierre. The languid Peninsular children
are home by midnight, and to the tipped glass of the

princess

I say, *The land-claims: I want to know.* Her mouth
opening like an osprey's:
*My father, my father! The pastel spirit-boats
of the dead--*

The Kenai spun into the Aleutians towards Siberia.
There were whitecaps and Beluga whales,
a circle of wolves, the sun lifting like this
over the hundred-mile river of colorless peaks
and a thin red line of hunters--
We were having another drink.
The princess' face shone like tungsten because
her father was dead and her children
tumbled under the eye of the satellite-fed television
in bright snow falling.

Polarity

A father loves him with careful pressure.
The mother stays unfocused, her face
blurred with indefinite pain.
His closest friend is afraid
of the inevitable loss coming, and lovers
open and close like the mouths of angelfish,
their bodies hitting and hitting at the glass.

He wants to break down, or out--
has so much love to account for.
In his own stunned way he's becoming a man.
Then let him cover the ground passionately
with timothy and sedge and prickly pear,
his own things. He will lie down in these
and think sometimes of the earth
on its heavy pivot: the heart,
the gravity of the manzanita.

Love in the Western World

Think of family, Ulster Irish
run out on a ram's horn,
our first real move.
The same square hands
ploughing through Missouri
and Iowa and Minnesota,
where we learned to muffle
the cavities of the body,
batten the heart down
on loneliness. Still it beats
family, family, as if the pulse
of our one-to-a-body rivers
ever ran singular. And if nothing
continues--the body ending
in this fist, everything short
of the mark--what do we want?
Don't give me history. No bridges
from my heart to your heart
to all of them stringing back
like dark berries: only
open my hand, press it
for the feel of the river,
the old fishline unreeling again.

Tess Gallagher

Unsteady Yellow

I went to the field to break
and to bury my precious things.
I went to the field
with a sack and a spade,
to the cool field alone.

All that he gave me
I dashed and I covered.
The glass horse, the necklace,
the live bird with its song, with
its wings like two harps--
in the ground, in the damp ground.

Its song, when I snatched it again
to air, flung it with light
over the tall new corn, its pure joy
must have reached him.

In a day it was back, my freed bird
was back. Oh now, what will I do,
what will I do with its song
on my shoulder, with its heart
on my shoulder when we come to
the field, to the high yellow field?

Conversation with a Fireman from Brooklyn

He offers, between planes,
to buy me a drink. I've never talked
to a fireman before, not one from Brooklyn
anyway. Okay. Fine, I say. Somehow
the subject is bound to come up, women
firefighters, and since I'm
a woman and he's a fireman, between
the two of us, we know something
about this subject. Already
he's telling me he doesn't mind
women firefighters, but what
they look like
after fighting a fire, well
they lose all respect. He's sorry, but
he looks at them,
covered with the cinders of someone's
lost hope, and he feels disgust, he just
wants to turn the hose on them, they
are that sweaty and stinking, just like
him, of course, but not the woman he
wants, you get me? and to come to that--
isn't it too bad, to be despised
for what you do to prove yourself
among men
who want to love you, to love you,
love you.

Each Bird Walking

Not while, but long after he had told me,
I thought of him, washing his mother, his
bending over the bed and taking back
the covers. There was a basin of water
and he dipped a washrag in and
out of the basin, the rag
dripping a little onto the sheet as he
turned from the bedside to the nightstand
and back, there being no place

on her body he shouldn't touch because
he had to and she helped him, moving
the little she could, lifting so he could
wipe under her arms, a dipping motion
in the hollow. Then working up from
the feet, around the ankles, over the
knees. And this last, opening
her thighs and running the rag firmly
and with the cleaning through
up through her crotch, between the lips
over the V of thin hairs--

as though he were a mother
who had the excuse of cleaning to touch
with love and indifference
the secret parts of her child, to graze
the sleepy sexlessness in its waiting
to find out what to do for the sake

of the body, for the sake of what only
the body can do for itself.

So his hand, softly at the place
of his birth-light. And she, eyes deepened
and closed in the dim room.
And because he told me her death as
important to his being with her,
I could love him another way. Not
of the body alone, or of its making,
but carried in the white spires of trembling
until what spirit, what breath we were
was shaken from us. Small then,
the word *holy*.

He turned her on her stomach
and washed the blades of her shoulders, the
small of her back. "That's good," she said,
"That's enough."

On our lips that morning, the tart juice
of our mothers, so strong in remembrance, no
asking, no giving, and what you said, this
being the end of our loving, so as not to hurt
the closer one to you, made me look
to see what was left of us
with our sex taken away. "Tell me," I said
"something you can't forget." Then the story of
your mother, and when you finished
I said, "That's good, that's enough."

The Ballad of Ballymote

We stopped at her hut
on the road to Ballymote
but she did not look up
and her head was on her knee.

What is it, we asked.
As from the dreams of the dead
her voice came up.

My father, they shot him
as he looked up from his plate
and again as he stood and again
as he fell against the stove
and like a thrush his breath
bruised the room
and was gone.

A traveler would have asked directions
but saw she would not lift her face.
What is it, he asked.

My husband sits all day in a pub
and all night and I may as well
be a widow for the way he beats me
to prove he's alive.

What is it, said the traveler's wife
just come up to look.

41

My son's lost both eyes in a fight
to keep himself a man
and there he sits behind the door
where there is no door
and he sees by the stumps
of his hands.

And have you no daughters for comfort?

Two there are and gone to nuns
and a third to the North
with a fisherman.

What are you cooking?

Cabbage and bones, she said. Cabbage
and bones.

The Ritual of Memories

When your widow had left the graveside
and you were most alone
I went to you in that future
you can't remember yet. I brought
a basin of clear water where no tear
had fallen, water gathered like grapes
a drop at a time
from the leaves of the willow. I brought

oils, I brought a clean white gown.

"Come out," I said, and you came up
like a man pulling himself out of a river,
a river with so many names
there was no word left for it but "earth."

"Now," I said, "I'm ready. These eyes
that have not left your face
since the day we met, wash these eyes.
Remember, it was a country road
above the sea and I was passing
from the house of a friend. Look
into these eyes where we met."

I saw your mind go back through the years
searching for that day and finding it,
you washed my eyes
with the pure water

so that I vanished from that road
and you passed a lifetime
and I was not there.

So you washed every part of me
where any look or touch
had passed between us. "Remember,"

I said, when you came to the feet,
"It was the night before you would ask
the girl of your village to marry. I
was the strange one. I was the one
with the gypsy look.
Remember how you stroked these feet."

When the lips and the hands
had been treated likewise and the pit
of the throat where one thoughtless kiss
had fallen, you rubbed in the sweet oil
and I glistened like a new-made thing, not
merely human, but of the world gone past
being human.

"The hair," I said. "You've forgotten
the hair. Don't you know it remembers.
Don't you know it keeps everything. Listen,
there is your voice and in it the liar's charm
that caught me."

You looked. You heard your voice
and a look of such sadness
passed over your dead face that I wanted
to touch you. Who could have known
I would be so held? Not you
in your boyish cunning; not me
in my traveler's clothes.

It's finished.
Put the gown on my shoulders.
It's no life in the shadow of another's joys.
Let me go freely now.
One life I have lived for you. This one
is mine.

From Dread in the Eyes of Horses

Eggs. Dates and camel's milk.
Give this. In one hour the foal will
stand, in two will run. The care then of
women, the schooling from fear, clamor
of household, a prospect of saddles.

They kneel to it, folded
on its four perfect legs, stroke
the good back, the muscles bunched at the chest.
Its head, how the will shines large in it
as what may be used to overcome it.

The women of the horses comb out
their cruel histories of hair only for
the pleasure of horses, for the lost mares
on the Ridge of Yellow Leaves, their white arms
praying the hair down breasts ordinary

as knees. The extent of their power,
this intimation of sexual wealth. From dread
in the eyes of horses are taken their songs.
In the white forests the last free horses
eat branches and roots, are hunted like deer
and carry no one.

A wedge of light where the doorway opens
the room--in it, a sickness of sleep.
The arms of their women, their coarse

46

white hair. In a bank of sunlight, a man
whitewashes the house he owns--no shores, no
worlds above it and farther, shrill, obsidian,
the high feasting of the horses.

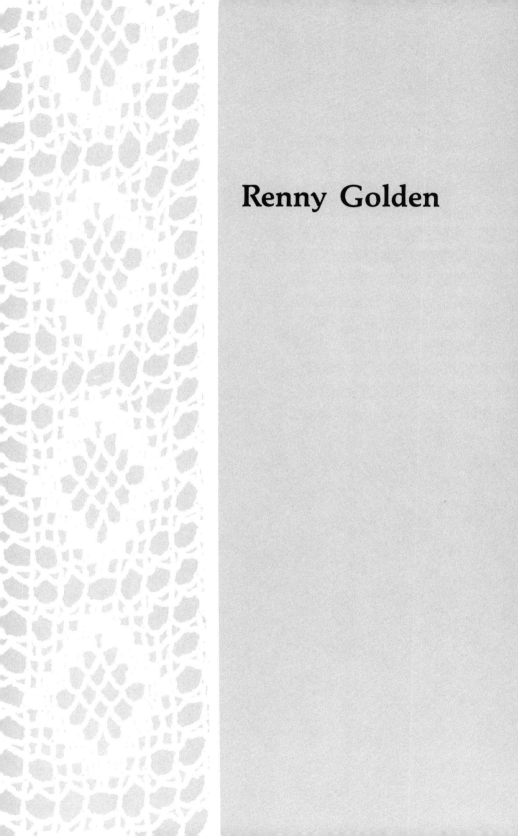

Renny Golden

Dinny Murphy

After his stroke his mouth sagged.
Defiant he'd drag his rag doll leg to work.
The union needed him less with these final wounds.
But long ago in both their green years
   he suffered a worker's lot.
Came home to my grandmother
   with dark mats of blood in his red hair,
watched Chicago police shoot down
   eleven steelworkers.

Stroke be damned missus, we'll see Kerry in the spring.
Then a Milwaukee sanitorium,
uproar and ranting, never slept away from the missus
   wouldn't now.
His daughters drove him, guilty at his trapped silence,
a wild old dog sensing his caged fate.
The poor mouth dropping, the eyes forlorn as his old collie.
In the end, led where he would not go,
he journeyed further than their pleas could reach him.
My mother said at the hospital he would not stop crying.

My grandmother, instinctual as a swallow
   to the Dingle coast,
drove down the night her thoughts on a young Irishman,
   flaming red hair
and the divil in his eye. Dinny.
When she arrived at midnight they clutched
   like lost children.

Weeping still he told what only he knew,
I'll not see Kerry in spring, missus.

The loss began then, those years I watched
   my grandmother;
sometimes at Christmas with grandchildren
   flapping around her
like blackbirds, her children's voices silver bells.
In the midst she'd turn as if suddenly
   missing someone,
puzzled for seconds that he was not there.

Until We're All Saints and Revolutionaries

Twenty years ago
I wanted to know a saint,
now it's a revolutionary.
Someone who means the part
about losing your life to find it.
Right now, you'll have to do.
Uncomfortable, huh?
Admiration has stung me too.
I've looked away, jaws gripping
until the reddening words stopped.
This insight is not false,
it's only putting it in words that's silly.
How we love each other,
long in the bones
for someone who isn't estimating,
walking, like Ruth, away from home
again and again.
My Naomi shouldn't embarass you.
This poem will touch
what I refuse.
My body is lucid,
but like all social constructions
it is both promise and problem.
But my eyes are free.
My eyes listen like a faithful dog.
They repeat a dog's interest.
If you could be here now,
my eyes would lick your hands.

Chicago to Boston: An April Lovesong

1

I come from the heartland bearing a wheat shaft,
limp marker of the times between.
In your garden I touch daffodils
shy as my first communion picture.
I tell you of winter, prisons,
and the ice palace of my work.
When my lament grinds,
the sound of gear stripping,
I come to the point.
Look, I don't frighten easily,
women like swollen magnolias will burst forth
lucid as a twilight sky after rain.
You see my hope's necessity is simple as the sadness
you softly brush away.
You are no magician with this trick.
But it is mysterious,
is it not my friend,
this power you have?

2

I walk a sea wall in Marblehead.
Forsythia bushrolls flutter from moss stone.
Bay winds shake dingys and snipes.
Gusts ring all harbor bells
clamorous as an Easter vigil's "Gloria."
Sea chimes and salty cliffs are not sufficient.
In your presence my stiffness twists away

like a somersaulting cat.
The body responds deep, silent as sun.
Hiked shoulders release to wings.
I stretch to gulls,
fingertip a ledge of blue, first foothills of sky,
perfect weave of flesh and skyborn bones.

The Quality of Mercy

1

What you notice is innocence
as if the suffering were not standing
holding her hand like an exhausted child.
Why doesn't she cry out?
It is almost unbearable.
She said I remind her of one who
came to her highland village
to teach cooperative farming.
Instinctively I want to be someone else,
someone dark, whose hands
smell of earth and oranges.

    After we organized the soldiers came.

I want to scream, somewhere a parrot screeches.

    We were running. The helicopters shooting
    into the woods. Lupe's huipil was all blood.
    At the ravine she said, I am not able, take
    my child.

I think it is finished and I breathe.
But her voice draws back
pushing a last sorrow into
the wind's dusty air chamber.
Exhausted, obedient I follow

her eyes to the infant suckling
the dark rose of her breast.

She is Lupe, and my son Enrique burned
with his father that morning.

Her face is impassive, years
of light drawn up into the *altiplano;*
the Sierras in the blue, cold distance.
In her open palm shadows gather dark
as the hour of the inferno.

She does not weep.
I try but tears splash
on my senseless hands.
She is a shy Indian woman,
I am only her second *gringa,*
but she holds my hand.
In that silence she watches
the cooking fires
die away in the fading light.
A dog barks in the distance;
Camp Chupadera hushes into
the purple night.

Compassion is not inexhaustible;
the heart, a small beast watching,
can change. A tiger in the breast, ready.
Courage is an animal with hungry cubs.

2

This has all happened before,
on Peterboro Street in Detroit, 1967.
All night long running, and
glass shattering, shouts snapping
the darkness like fireflies
or sparks. By dawn
we heard Anna Mae, in a
voice we'd never heard before:

> *Tell them they goin now, heah.*
> *Use they car and get to Wyandotte*
> *where they got a real convent*
> *'way nuns 'spose, not no nasty place...*

But she wouldn't come over.
past a barricade of garbage cans,
we saw her on the stoop cradling
baby Lilly, stiff, remote as a bronze Pieta.
Morning framed her intentions, showering
petals of light on her shoulders, the infant.
But it was not a Southern morning,
the air sweet with wild gardenias.
A faint smell of gasoline was everywhere.
As we circled past a squad car,
she stood into that crackling air,
her faded flowered housecoat

luminous in the sunlight.
That final picture of Anna Mae,
the old dress with bleached pink magnolias.

The quality of mercy is measured
in those final moments before
the hour of fire.

Sheila, A Friend Distracted by History

You don't arrange
yourself
like plucked daffodils
into an open palm of attentiveness.
It is not willful
your half measure of interest,
as if distant music
echoing long reaches
of grass fields
pulled you through the window
into a blue Chagall sky.
I listen hard,
expect European violins,
but is is a chorus:
Mississippi, Nicaraguan, South African accents
ringing like a chisel against
the granite statue of Law,
the grey stone safety of white skin.
Then softer, the ancient refrain of the people,
melodious as rain twirling wheat from rock soil.
The song of the poor,
you never tire of it,
leaning into the stars
outside your bedroom window
listening.
The people's music burning
night candles in the
black holes of history,

singing in many tongues again and again,
this one song:
vinceremous,
we shall overcome.

The children dance or tumble
for your attention, tears are best.
But at dinner tables, restaurants,
you barely listen anymore.
The other voices singing
from Jalapa, Huehuetenanogo,
Tchula, Morazon.
Sometimes far from home,
with twilight's mortal light
inviting your deep attention,
I think you, shining in the new light,
have become the song.

For a Revolutionary Returning to Peru

Balsam branches
take flame bare
as an open hand
light as snow.
From shadows your
voice heavy in
pine scent tells
of choices hanging
ripe as berries
on winterwood.
How you pluck your
life from the fragrant air.
I watch your
hands rise like
geese to your
voice's call.
Ember sparks
are cat eyes
in darkness.
For you passion
has no coals,
only this flaming.

Ethna McKiernan

Biographical Notes

Described once as the mother of none
Caught me flat: as if I were that, and only that.
I think I blustered, "No--yes--but--wait,
Aunt of 23, sister of nine; wife of one;"
Etc., etc., before I could help myself.

Suppose I were a stone: no pedigree,
Total anonymity. Unless centuries of history
Burned their mark on me and so bore claim
Of some legitimacy
In the definition of that stone.

Not being stone, mornings
I just brush my hair and check the sky
For news of who I am,
What liner notes to sum me up today.
An ordinary woman with no children,

I eat cantelope and words for breakfast,
And on the bus I read again, this time
Weary novels in the sad riders' eyes.
Damn your definitions: what possible
Compressed assembly of parts or motion

Can distill a pretty kernel representing all?
Evenings, checking the street for strangers,
I unlock the storefront door
And gladly step into my own warm glossary,

Shedding layers of a rigid world's hand.

But some nights, some nights, daughter
Whom I've never known, poetry descends
Right throught the leaking roof
And swarms inside my brain
Like honey in a golden river,

Wild-currented in spring, splashing
Smooth, silent stones.
And it is then, only then,
I could tell you
Exactly who I am.

Morning Revelations from the Cosmos

I know what the black wires mean
Against the pale fire sky
With one bird astride the wires
Precisely where they verge.

I know, too, the frail garden parsley
Must endure its placement
Near the chalk-bone blue of broccoli
The worms have chewed.

All this knowing makes my backbone sway
A bit, and the ground somewhat unsteady;
Like opening the lid to the world's great core
And breathing the power that smolders there.

But God must choose the chosen
Carefully, and so he tests the depths of wisdom
Coursing through my blood, hurling out
Tongues of riddles, faster and faster

They babble from grooves in tree bark,
Buzz and swoop through hidden airwaves
Of the morning, chatter slyly
From the very blades of grass underfoot.

But I know. I know
Each foreign word, each holy note
The one black bird whistles from his perch
Upon the wires up above. I know. I know.

One Summer's Lake

This is no lake,
It's a flat blue egg. We peel
Its shell and climb inside
Like four spoons looking for the yolk.

Or else it is a mirror,
Giving us only half the truth.
We'll dive for the rest,
Cutting the bevel sideways
With a slice.

What surrounds us now?
The moon is a crazy rustler,
Rounding up the news.
Water-echoes bounce us remnants,
All the daily gossip.

And now we rise, four
Alabaster bodies playing statues.
You are a tropical bird,
Grave and lovely,
Lifting a wing to the sky.

You say: Look, the moon
Is a stained-glass belly,
A pregnant melon. Tonight

It will drop an infant moon
For each of us.

Nobody speaks. Your laugh
Swims back to shore.

Going Back

Here: it must be where you stood,
One hand raised to shade your eyes
Against the harsh Atlantic
Grinding shoulders with the rocks below.

How your skirt cut the wind in half!
And how you waited, brooding
For the boats that stitched their slow way in
With ribboned wakes a deeper green,
And each new ship
A promise that you couldn't keep.

I see the girl you were
Walk back alone to her father's house,
Caught between two hungers.
Some absent strain of music kept you restless,
And I know how the longing worked on you,
For even at night
The boats sent out a siren tongue--
Foreign to your ear, perhaps, but song.

One day you finally left,
Sailing your boat straight into the cave
Of America's open arms;
Feeling the wind no monster
There, after such lean dreams
As you had culled from Irish soil.

Mama Mor, I stand here now
Where you once stood,
The unchanged land beneath my feet,
Certain that my bones were formed
From that same air
That made your bones first stir.

But the old heritage
Breeds a different pain in me:
A stranger to both countries,
I cannot make my roots take hold;
Can only stand and hear the sea
Return the poems that you'd willed it
As a child, while the wind
Raises ghosts behind me.

The Other Woman

You visit her house for the first time without him.
She offers you tea, a still-warm jar of raspberry jam,
Kindness to trouble your insides.
Later you walk outdoors into the perfect garden,
And it is too clear that the apple trees
Have been tended carefully for years,
For they are verging on their first green fruit.
Everything here, in fact, has roots.

Inside now her children fan about her
Like blue stones in a peacock's upraised tail,
And every facet of each gem
Throws back his reflection, too.
It is too beautiful, too cruel.

At night he comes to you once more
And you are not innocent,
Knowing precisely where
To place your hands upon his back
While he breaks his loneliness inside you.

So you hold him, you hold his past, you hold
The faint shadow of his wife
Which staggers there between you,
You hold a gift of jam
And an empty, outstretched hand
Awake, thinking of her,
Even as she thinks of you.

Two Poems for Naoise

1

First one, little fish,
You kick and dart and glide
Beneath my ribs
As if they were your private reef.

For months I've felt you fatten
Like a mollusk,
Each swell and bump of you
A new pearl.

Sea-newt, limpet-child
I've never known,
I am your mother ocean:
My arms are waves

Holding you, I rock
Your tiny bones
Inside the brine.
Sleep here; you're home.

2

The dark hums like dim thunder at this hour.
It is still and black, so black
Naoise, that your pale face shines
Like a nugget of light at my breast

Even your veins work bright ridges
On your head as you suck.

How many centuries have women
Stared into the blue night like this,
Wondering at such helplessness
As yours, as sounds of distant soldiers
Edged closer home through street or field?
Centuries or continents away, Belfast

Or Beruit, they do not cease. Nursing you
Like this is such sweet peace
Some days it seems just random luck,
Miraculous as the juggler's caught ball
Or the car that slowly left the market
Just before the bomb. That your pink mouth

Spills drowsy milk and you sleep again
Makes me humble. Perhaps the world
Is more benign that I believe. Tiny one,
I don't know. I hold you tightly
To me, knowing in Chernobyl yesterday
Another child has died.

Postscript: My Lai

My daughter is dead.

The flame at the center
No longer burns; the wind wails
Lost and broken through the hut.

When it was over,
I wanted to strangle in grief.
They told me peace would come with sleep,

But each time I closed my eyes
I saw her face explode a thousand times
And heard her scream out "mother."

Now blood chokes the rice paddies,
And only bones float up
To greet the harvest.

My daughter is dead.

Katherine
McNamara

The Scythe-Sharpener

The sun tips past noon,
        aslope to the west.
His house eyes you: it's time.
His shirt of pins bristles,
his stone sparks.
The blade is nearly honed.
He will cut
a handful:
        Grass.
        A throat.

The Rower

Gold September,
        gold light of Tuscany
on the Arno. I watch
        a single rower
in his spidery shell.
        He moves through water
and air so perfectly,
        in such fine measure, that
his strokes are calm breathing.

I still see the slim
        white wake,
the broadening waves
        in that opaque water,
that gilt light. He is always
        just passing the window.
I turn my head so slightly left,
        to keep him
in clear sight.

Entwined, And Fleeing

We are here a pair of loons
their long necks curved and swooping
I at your shoulder, you at my thigh
and as all fleet lovers do (these birds
who filled the tree-topped air above us)
our eyes -- o, your cursive eyes --
fall away   follow the slope of the hill
glide into those trees clothed in flowers --
dogwood *cup of light in the woods*, redbud
curling in the groin
of smooth-barked branches --
twinning, our eyes desperate and set
on one another then look smoothly, apart,
from tree to tree, they turn swift
and dart, like these little and big birds
in pairs, with longing:
If we could fly! as they fly!

The Magic Drunk

1

Needing sweeter sound
I take the piece of bone and scrape it
smooth it
suck out the marrow
make myself a whistle,
a charm.
And, touching it like a lover's face,
I find a song of grace and ease
to keep at bay the dread voice
at the edge of the circle of my song.

2

That voice is the magic drunk
He promises purity
a region of peace behind his eyes
He lies

3

I took you with me to a cabin; we were cut off
by trees around us and, beyond them,
by waves of green and purple mountains
lapping at our own mountain.
To our pleasure, we heard the beautiful tones of a gong
of three sides, each side speaking a different deep
thrilling voice, the voice of a nun

praying calmly in her cell, behind walls.
High in the branches hung a wolverine's skull,
his jaws voracious. 'He's still hunting,' you said.

These were your only wise words.
I should have left you. You were a drunkard.
I loved you. He was hunting me.

4
I knew a man. He knew how to place his hands
on a woman. The light is green, the air
melodious with birds, I am the slave of lust.
Sprawled, unclothed, I can conjure up
hands on narrowed eyelids, a name,
I mouth, I tongue it, sensing
he will come here
in August, when it's hotter,
when the air is dusty,
and rasps with locusts.

If I think of you it is not as my lover.

5
And these were the signs of all our sorrows:
that the heat licked at the door of this house
with its dry tongue, that the songbirds stopped their songs.
You fled to your room, where you drew
powerful animals on the wall. You called the animals,
and the fire licked at the door.

6

Your drunken eyes drive even me away.
Now you turn to face the animals.
At night they move down from the paintings
to surround you in your room. And across town
as hard as my hands press my ears
I hear you scream and scream, a wild horse
frothing at the binding rein
as they light torches
and fire the grass around you.

7

The leaves begin their gossip, idle tongues.
Now the breath sighs, up and down the hill
the leaves whisper behind their hands . . .
Now the air grows still. What is this fever?
A shadow flicks against my eyelid.
The sky answers in rhyme.
A laugh deep in the throat, thunder.
If only I could breathe. If I could hold my breath
long enough the storm would come
leaping and growling in the hills,
the fire pools melt into green mirrors.

                                        The storm
prowls and growls on the hills.
I stand at the door. Wait. Flick, flick
of eyelid
The shadow

The growl
The eye's lightning!
The breath of the world sighing on me
The rain wants me, the thunder wants me
The lightning leaps to show itself to me!
I am the storm's lover
It casts its shadow on my eyelid
Am I dreaming? Am I dreaming? Am I dreaming?

The Grave Digger

The old spells are lost. A few words
stick in his mouth, broken teeth.
His pelt bristles with pins.

I will dig for you. O, are you not tired?
(When may I lay my own head down?) I will dig
and keep digging for you.

Patricia Monaghan

West County

Nine ponies wheel againt the lower wall,
the choreography of Connemara.
Needing them near, we call and call and call.

The summer night reels with approach of fall.
We know that we'll be going north tomorrow.
Ponies wheel against an Irish wall.

We want to touch them once, to feel how tall
they stand, to share their fleshy sorrow.
Needing them near, we call and call and call.

But they remain across the field, all animal
intensity, so pure and so amoral.
Ponies wheel against the lower wall.

Like crazy beggars now we sing in thrall
to that fierce freedom that is Connemara
there in horses who ignore our call--

and now the wheel rolls towards us, all
we might have wished, all fury there to borrow.
Nine ponies wheel against the upper wall.
We need this nearness. Call and call and call.

Ballinduff

1

Working the hayfield, you recite
the old words, necessary facts:
sop and *bart*, rake to the right;
tram, cock, rick, pile up the stacks.

The divisions of the hay
become familiar as I fall
into the rhythm of the day,
the reach, the lift, the haul.

2

You are not the stranger here. You know
the country words for everything you see:
boreen, the road beside the cottage door;
turlough, the winter lakes that pour
frogs into the garden. You teach me
that *haggard* means--not weary, no--
the henstained flagstone yard.
You laugh, schoolmasterly. It isn't hard.

3

This evening after haying

trams stand in the field
under a white sky

and why

last night beneath the braying
moon had you no words to wield
as you gathered me, less than gently?
Where were the old words then,
the soundings of a common time
when love was measured differently?

For we have no way to claim
what lies between us now
no words precise enough to name
what fills our meadows,
splendid, still, unmeasured--
and so it will remain.

In County Mayo

The turf settles as we again assign
blame for the unfathomable, cousins
in a house perishing with loss: sons
prisoned or dead, the border at hand,
a war at table, wounded mother,
father poisoned with clarity. My left
leg scalds from the blaze, my right
is numb from a doorway breeze.

It is one a.m. Hot and damp in a crowded
bedroom, Ita coughs and calls from
the other bed. Over here, secret forces
evade the grip of security police;
there is a plot to overthrow
the government and counter attempts
to unmask sixteen conspirators.
These dreams are as familiar as cousins
and jumprope rhymes, and strange
as an old land finally visited.

It was too easy when I said
there were things I might die for
but I did not know if I could kill.
The dreams, the dreams. This split
island and its wars, grandfather
songs, *glory-o, glory-o,* and
cousins stories, legacy of night.

The Rebel Dreams

You were always running, trying to place
phone calls to missing members or, in the worst
case, to the authorities. When you were caught
in public with your coded messages, you claimed
you found them in vending machines, you claimed
no knowledge of revolt, you claimed and claimed
until you killed yourselves or turned traitor.

Once I remember the police bursting into
your castellated hideout, all of them armed
with glistening iron, all of you nailing
yourselves to the walls with suicide arrows.

After that, disguised as a mime troupe,
you entertained at fairs and rituals, but
the glances exchanged among you made it clear
the plots went on, the reasons for rebellion
had become traditional, skits and ballads now,
certain habits of clothing and tatooing.
You even talked to me once, on the sidewalk,
in undisguised terms of the significance
of whiteface, but then blindfolded me and
held me captive at the spider-temple while you
discussed assassination as a theatrical device.

Now you appear in leather and bikers' helmets
and bulldoze my forest to landscape a lawn

with Louis Quatorze filligrees of snapdragons
and azaleas, and of course I recognize you,

and know that next you'll return disguised
as unemployed farmers protesting flowerbeds
where crops could grow and placing scarecrows
oddly along the rows, and that crows will then
roost there in despite, and that the crows will be
yet another disguise, one with wings, for you.

Hiroshima Mon Amour

When they touch hands
it is a treaty, an
entreaty, between

continents: your father
left Poland just in time,
my grandfather left Ireland
just in time, your father
was not exterminated,
my grandfather did not
become an assassin--

Have you ever been marched
down the street in Nevers,
shorn for love? Have you
never? The forlorn lovers

on the screen entreat
each other's trust; beside
you the German woman,
beside me, the English man--
Hiroshima, Hi-ro-shi-ma--
we know nothing, nothing at all,
we do not even always understand
the language, we do not even
always understand, and the Laotian
behind us whispers the meaning:

Have you ever been marched
down the street in Nevers,
shorn for love? Have you
never?   Your father would have

spit in the eye of the German
woman, my grandfather would have
refused to sit beside the English
man, that Laotian behind us
is translating a poison tongue,

how much we have reason to hate,
how much reason there is to be guilty,
how much reason there is to hate us

--sitting together in the dark--

when we touch hands
it is an entreaty

One of Us is Missing

Which one of the babies ran away that day?
No one can remember but we all recall
some toddler adventuring in diapers down
the rollerskate sidewalk or through
the lilacs or maybe onto the gravel path
leading to Jeannette's cherry grove.

It could have been any of us. Sisters
beneath the cottonwoods we would sometimes
fall into the old dry pools that once held
goldfish, sometimes fall from trees we were
forbidden to climb, sometimes find ourselves
trapped in old barns behind the old houses
where the old folks lived. It could have been anyone.

We remember only the search. Surely there was
joy when this lost sheep was found, surely there was
celebration at our wholeness, surely we rejoiced that
all of us were there, that none of us was missing, but no one
can remember it. And one of us, surely, was that child,

but each of us remembers searching, searching,
no one remembers either being lost or being
found, no one remembers anyone being found,
not that time or ever, not ever, not at all.

That was twenty years ago. This week we are together,
we share a hotel in Manhattan, we are all
safe and sound, we have all escaped our
childhoods, we shop, we sightsee, we keep
turning and counting, someone is missing,
we are all together but someone has always
just walked off, someone has disappeared.

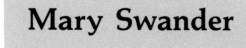

Mary Swander

Quay

The boat is waiting
far out in the harbor.
There is a man on board,
leaning over the railing,
a woman standing on the dock,
her black shawl wrapped
around her shoulders,
her head, her red petticoat
showing just beneath her knees.
She is not weeping.
She is not even waving.
Her small white handkerchief
is tucked into her sleeve.
She does not wait to watch the mast
disappear into the sea.
She does not huddle together with the other women
like the swans
trying to squeeze the first bit of morning
heat from the rocks
on the shore.
She turns and walks on
past the market where the pig's knuckles
and black and white puddings
are packed in ice,
and the fish scales
glow purple as small coals.
There she stops and
blows on her hands.

She looks back.
Along the bay she sees
horses running wild
among the cattle,
boys in blue shirts
playing with a ball
along the sand.
A dog trots
across the horizon.
The daffodils and whinbush
are just flowering.
There is the smell of peat
burning, blackening the chimneys.
The grass is very green.

For Mary Lynch

The white cement walls, thatched roof,
the rose bush blooming just outside, the small table
inside next to your rocker -- it all looked so familiar.

And over the hearth, the picture of the Virgin's heart,
the layers of flesh torn away, the bramble
of thorns twisted around the fist-shaped muscle.

And the picture of your father, his fields
dried up, the potatoes shriveled to the size
of your fingers, then curled back into the earth,

everyone else gone and relatives
there at the tip of Inishmore, "the isle of tears,"
taking one last look at the ships leaving.

That night I found you in the old church
kneeling alone, hands folded, your white hair
wet with rain, pressed under a woolen scarf,

the soft light of the votive candle blurring
your face, and I could feel the weight of your body,
of a whole family, fall away, dissolve as if a thin wafer.

The next morning we ate breakfast together:
eggs, scones, tea; brown bread and strawberry jam.
Then half way down the road, I turned and waved,

the ship's bell clanging. You stood there by the bush,
the sun shining into the house, your one hand
raised, the fingers, blossoms, curled open.

Sea-Woman

She sat in the boat, huddled beneath the bow, head down, knees bent, her arms wound around her shins. It was a cool May afternoon and the wind blew along the lake and the sails flapped and her tiny red scarf flapped against her head. She reached up and tightened the knot. Then she pulled me closer and for a moment I too became afraid of the water, of a storm, of tipping the boat over. She never learned how to swim. I wanted to get up, to leave her, to sit in the middle of the boat with my father and brothers. I wanted to guide the rudder, to lower the mast, swing the sails, ropes, leaning my whole body toward the water. But I stayed down there beneath the bow with her.

And she told me stories. In the old days in Ireland, she said, men made small boats from one cow's skin. They stretched the hide over laths and sewed a long seam. The boat was weightless like a basket. It would skim out over the water -- the safest thing on the sea. The fishermen in currachs received medals for saving other larger craft caught on the rocks. And in the old days, she said, if you were a bad sinner, they put you in a currach and set you out to sea with no food, water, oars.

And some of these fishermen traced their descent back to the sea-woman. She appeared one day on shore as a seal, took off her skin and became a lovely woman. A young man saw her, stole her skin and she followed him home where he dressed her in ordinary clothes and she forgot about the sea.

105

The young man married her and they had three children and all went well until one day when the youngest child found a strange bundle hidden in the barn and brought it to her mother who recognized her sealskin and remembered her own people and life at sea. Then she said good-bye to her children, put on the skin and slipped under the waves and never again came on land, although she often swam on the surface just off shore, talking and singing to her children.

And each night I sat beside her bed, I wanted to rock her. I wanted to leave her. She called my name and I came to her and she thought me her mother, she thought me her father, the doctor. She called my name and I came to her but I wanted to turn back like a fisherman seeing a red-haired woman on his way to sea. I wanted to stay there beside her and sing to her. I saw myself floating away with her, a sinner, wrapped in her skin.

Song

And each night was a vigil:
the moon, the two small candles beside your bed, the only light.
And the wicks burning, traveling through your body, the needle,
the long strings, the green mold boring a hole through the bread.

And the wax melting, the thin wax lips taking you in, the hollow,
the cup, your lung filling, draining . . .

And the flames rising, hanging in the air, were tongues
inside bells ringing the hours: one, one;
tongues inside your body when I was there.

And the moon, rising over your bed, was a host.
And your body was eaten.

Succession

It doesn't matter if the light fails.
Tonight, my fingers move automatically
Along the rows, each stitch
As familiar as a bead of the rosary.

I simply follow the family pattern
My Irish grandmothers knit into sweaters
For their sons, the fine threads
Spun off the skulls of Nordic sailors.

And when I stop to raise my hands,
It will be in the way of a priest
Blessing boats. I'll poke my arms
Through the dark and listen

For the clack of needles, oars.
I'll prostrate myself on the floor,
Let down the nets, the great walls
Of the house, and float out,

The tides, the full moon, a tangle
Of yarn, pulling me in, cell by cell,
My flesh unraveling, all revealing
Marks gone: scars, face, fingerprints,

My whole body the shore by dawn.

Nancy Sarah
Schoellkopf

How to Find the Muse

Think about the sky.

It's a new blue tablecloth
and a big-hipped woman
has carelessly dribbled
gobs of whipped cream
all over it.

There she has set down
an orange bowl.
Smell cinnamon and coriander
as you scoop
spicy carrots
and squash from the bowl
to your mouth.
Bite into a raw cucumber
to cool the fiery curry
on your tongue.

Now drum your fingertips
on the table.
Listen to a jazz quartet.
Tap your feet
on a black and white
tiled floor.
When she starts to sing

those torchy blues
press your lips together
and hum
until you taste sweetened cream
spilling from the sky.

Headband

Suddenly leaves are red
sky is pink
and you sit
at a midtown bus stop
hands thrust into the pockets
of your army-surplus jacket.
A woman approaches
her voice
a mountain stream
amid traffic
singing of the moon
and the string
that ties the stars together
as she bounces a baby
on her hip.
Now your mind will meander
through a summer meadow
following a humming bird
that flutters at her shoulder
attracted to her
red head
band.

Charmed Life

We trespass on this field
now dry with October thistles
that cling to denim cuffs
and cotton socks.
Last summer it was a green pasture
for brown and white cows
their baritone lowing
accompanied by heavy stone bells
round their necks.
Another season Miwok Indians
ambled over yellowing hills.
They did not claim the land
for it could not be owned
any more than one could own
the air as it vibrates
with shrill music
of magpies and rustling leaves
or the soft whistle of flutes fashioned
from the hollow bones of birds.

A narrow flood plain
is still green despite six dry months.
We eat cheddar cheese
and artichokes
speak of European parents
who marked time
on bone and reed
embroidered ballads

with horsehair bows.
After lunch you find
at water's edge
a long cow's rib
picked clean and white
by river's current.
You will add it to your collection
your spoons and your drum.

From a promise of rhythm
you will knit
a travelling cloak
trimmed with mossy lace.
It will warm you
though your head is bare
as you cast your hope
on the Cosumnes' south fork;
it carves billowing ribs
through the Amador hills.

Life On The Flood Plain

Nestled in the south elbow
of the levee
we are sheltered from the river
now swelling with melted snow
as it zigzags though this valley
like the roots of our apricot tree
stretching into the lawn.

Forced from a sandy burrow
by rising water
a lone jack rabbit
his ears a brown exclamation point
careens from street to sidewalk
seeking a shelter
amid juniper bushes and moss
where Saint Francis extends
a granite hand
beckoning sparrows to lunch
on discarded bread crust
Mom trimmed from our toast.

Inside two cats lounge
on a plastic table cloth
black limbs curled lazily
around an African violet
in a clay pot

and human babies
resolve to live forever
on Mom's cookie dough
and duets Dad sings with the dog.

Immigrant

1

Blades
not sharp or brutal
but tender
and yielding to the weight
of my bare feet
sprout
on this thin layer of soil
that hugs the Donegal coast.
I grasp a clump of green shoots
in my fist:
does that make it mine
or does it belong
to a middle-aged man
with a piece of paper
in London?
I pluck fuschia and rhododendron
that grow thick and wild
and perfume glides through my kitchen
spreading itself thinner and thinner
over the scent of boiling potatoes.
I dig in my root garden
glance at a sky bruised with purple longing.
This island is too small, I think,
its energy
a tremendous hawk
beating rapid wings

in a storm
panics, turns mean
when it has no place to light.

2

Set back from a craggy coast
in a warm California valley
two rivers merge
without roar of triumph
without pathetic yelp of subordination
but with a steady rush
a joyful tumble.
Even frustrated whirlpools
find release in concentric circles
rippling the surface.
Water laps against the river bank
in ambitious efforts to expand
and there is room
for the delta
to spread forceful fingers
like the blue grey feathers
of a heron's wings
stretching in graceful ascent.

Here the clawed feet of my apricot tree
gently grip the moist knuckles
of the flood plain
and orange blossoms
their waxy petals

impervious to early spring rains
survive to bestow a heady scent
on April mornings
splashing on my eyelids and cheeks
like tears
not hot with anger
but cool like the Sacramento River
swelling with melted snow.